CHRISTERIA LYNN

From Desperation to Destiny

Finding HOPE and INDEPEDENCE through Secret Struggles

From Desperation to Destiny

Finding HOPE and INDEPENDENCE through Secret Struggles

Christeria Lynn

Christeria Lynn, Atlanta, Georgia

Copyright © 2018 by Christeria Lynn

All rights reserved. No part of this book may be reproduced or transmitted in any form or by any means without written permission of the author. Reviewers may quote brief passages in reviews.

Neither the author nor the publisher assumes any responsibility for errors, omissions, or contrary interpretations of the subject matter herein. Any perceived slight of any individual or organizations is purely unintentional.

Brand and product names are trademarks or registered trademarks of their respective owners.

All names in this book have been changed to protect the identity of others.

Printed in the United States of America

Dedication

This book is dedicated to my six children and every person who ever felt less than good enough. Remember, you are still *destined*.

CONTENTS

Chapter 1: Against All Odds..8

Chapter 2: How Pain Purposed Me..17

Chapter 3: Hoping for a New Life..31

Chapter 4: Beaten and Broken...45

Chapter 5: Letter of the Broken Hearted................................57

Chapter 6: From Desperation to Destiny................................72

Chapter 7: P.E.A.C.E. 83

About the Author..111

1

Against All Odds

Born to a single mother named Lynn and a father named Ruby, I was given the name Christeria Lynn. I was such a beautiful baby girl by looking at my pictures. Born with pale skin, curly hair and pretty black eyes, I was the oldest of four girls. My mother was an alcoholic, and my father was nowhere to be found. My mother was a hard worker and strived to provide for her children. When I was growing up, we didn't have gas and electricity because it got turned off. We had to run a cord from an aunt's house, who lived next door to our house, so we could have electricity. On the days we weren't able to do that, we used flashlights to find our way.

Because we didn't have gas, we also didn't have hot water. We went to our aunt's house to boil water and would bring it back to our house to take a warm bath. I tried to internalize my feelings, but I didn't quite understand why children had to go through this. We had a big blue cooler that sat in the middle of our living room. That's where we stored our food when we didn't have gas and electricity. The cooler was full of ice and mostly cold cuts. While our meals may have been limited, we never went without a meal. My mother made sure we always ate, even if she couldn't provide utilities for us. At times, it felt like I was exhausted from being a child. When my mother wasn't around, I felt as if I was responsible for my little sisters. I felt like I had to do those things I wanted someone to do for me, for them. I made sure my siblings were always okay and that they were fed and taken care of.

Being the oldest child seemed like a blessing at the time. What I didn't realize is that being the oldest came with more responsibility and less independency. I didn't want either. I tried figuring out life at an early age, but it seemed too complicated. Taking care of children who weren't mine and bearing responsibilities that I shouldn't have to bear did nothing but make me angry. I wanted a childhood. I wanted a normal life. Instead of doing the things children longed to do, I had to do the things that parents should have been doing. Although it wasn't my job, someone had to do it. Deep down inside, I was hurting. I was wondering what my parents were thinking about. Maybe, they weren't thinking at all. How could parents make children and make everything else a priority, but the children? Deep down, I knew there had to be more to life than this.

Feeling rejected, abandoned, lost, confused and overwhelmed, I often asked myself, "What is this thing called life about?" I was raised in an apartment complex that my grandparents owned in a small community. Everyone knew everyone. One of my aunts lived in apartment number one and another one of my aunts lived in apartment number two, along with my uncle. A nice lady lived in apartment three, and we stayed in apartment four. Even though I was surrounded by immediate family, I still felt unloved. As a young child, I didn't understand what it meant to truly be loved. I didn't feel loved. I always prayed that God would just give me my mother and my father. My aunts and uncles, and my grandmother, filled in for my mother when she couldn't be there. Although I knew we didn't have much, I knew that we always had what I thought we needed.

Grandma's Grace

My grandmother was always at our house and my aunt's house. Grandma was there for all of her grandchildren and she played a huge role in my life. My grandmother loved Jesus. She went to church daily and often, I was right by her side. I was raised in Calvary United Methodist Church in Evanston. We attended church almost *every day*. If there was a funeral, we were there. If there was a church tea party, I was there with my grandmother. If there was an ushers' meeting, we were there. Sometimes, I wanted a break from church. I didn't understand why we had to go to church so much. I thought to myself, *I know God can hear what we are saying. How much more can we tell God?*

My grandmother always bought me the things I wanted. Oftentimes, the items were from a second-hand store, but they were mine. I understood what she bought me didn't have to be new, it just had to be appreciated. The simple fact that I was getting what I wanted is what mattered. My grandmother bought me a bunch of Barbie Dolls that came with toy swimming pools, motorcycles and doll houses. I really wasn't interested in them, but I was grateful to have them. I would rather play football outside with the guys and have a remote-controlled car, but I didn't want to be perceived as ungrateful. The mere fact that she took the time out to give me what she thought I wanted meant so much. She bought me a Strawberry Shortcake doll, which I fell in love with. It was something about the red-headed doll with freckles that was different. Strawberry Shortcake was different. That's when I realized that I was just as different. Strawberry Shortcake didn't look like any other doll that I'd seen, and neither did I. I just felt *different*. God eventually spoke to me and told me I was the golden child. I knew the golden child was different because I had seen the movie, *The Golden Child*. I didn't understand what my future would hold, but I felt like my life was going to be great. My early childhood is a reflection of a little girl who said she was loved but didn't feel loved and was confused about the love from her mother and father.

A Daughter's Broken Trust

On a warm, summer night, at the age of nine, my sister and I went to our bedroom to prepare for bed. My sister slept on the bottom bunk bed, and I slept on the top bunk. We wore our Strawberry Shortcake nightgowns with ruffles at the bottom to bed that night. My sister and I often conversed until we fell asleep. We wouldn't talk about much of anything, but mostly about what was going on at school and what we wanted to do the next day. Suddenly, I heard a noise.

I heard someone at the door and it sounded like our bedroom door was slowly opening. But it also seemed pretty late in the night. Something just didn't seem right. The door opened, and I saw a familiar face. I peeked and slightly opened my eyes. Then, I saw my stepfather standing next to the bed, hovering over me. His round head and receding hair line couldn't be mistaken for anyone else. He didn't say a word, but he saw that my eyes were open. I just laid there and cried in silence. He robbed me of what was special to me. I saw these kinds of stories on the news, but never imagined it would be part of my story. He put his fingers over his lips and said, "Shhhhh!" before sliding his fingers into my panties. "If you tell anyone, you will get in trouble. If you tell, I will deny it. No one will believe you anyway."

After he was finished with me, he went to the lower bunk bed. I don't remember my sister making a sound or even saying a word. It happened so late and so fast, yet it was eternally painful. I never imagined what deep pain an adult could bring to an innocent child. I thought to myself, *How can he do something like this to the children he claims to love*?

Looking back at the things that he did for me, it all made sense. He bought me things that he wouldn't buy anyone else, and he made me hide the things he bought me. For example, he knew I'd wanted a pink Coke shirt really bad. My stepfather took me to the store and purchased me a light pink and red shirt. But, when we got back to the house, he told me to hide it in my dresser drawer. Little did I know, I'd have to hide more than shirts.

The day after my sister and I had been violated, we talked about what our stepfather had done to us. We wondered if we should say something or not. *If we told our mother, would she even believe us?* He said she wouldn't. Having never met my biological father, and having a stepfather who violated me, I thought to myself, *Is this what men do to you? Do they just abandon you and violate you?* Not only did I feel the void of my missing biological father, but now I had to deal with the pain of what was now taken from me. The only man that I'd known as "daddy" violated me. I was so young, yet in so much pain.

As time progressed, I couldn't stand to look at him. I didn't want this to happen to me and my sister again, or anyone else for that matter. I cried. I asked myself questions. I even asked God questions but didn't seem to get any answers. Feeling antagonized by my feelings, it seemed like I was wearing the coat of guilt and shame. I couldn't take it any longer. The silent pain was eating away at me. I felt useless. I felt like someone had stripped me of my voice.

I mustered up enough strength and courage to tell my mother exactly what he had done to *us*. Of course, he denied it and told her that I was making up a story. She asked us several questions and I explained to her what happened, play by play. I explained it my mother over and over again, but she didn't believe me. I don't think she even heard me. The only father I'd ever known violated me, and the only mother I had didn't believe me. My mother told me, "You're making up stories and you should stop lying on people." She made me feel bad about what I was saying, as well as what had happened. Even though she denied the truth, it didn't change the truth. I never told anyone else until later on in life.

Until *now*.

I wanted to tell my grandmother, but I didn't want her to look at me like I was crazy. She probably wouldn't believe me either. To walk around, knowing that the woman who gave birth to me, wouldn't take the necessary steps to protect me was hard for me to grasp as a child. Tears flowed, my heart was broken, and my childhood was interrupted and shattered. The rejection and pain was growing deeper. *Daddy, where are you? Daddy, why did you leave me? Daddy, I need you to protect me. Daddy, please find me and come and get me.* For years, and now decades, I wondered where my father was and why he never tried to find me. The secret of the molestation left me devastated. From that point on, I didn't trust anyone. Life would go on, as if nothing ever happened. Rejection, abandonment, violation and broken trust were my new norms.

2

How Pain Purposed Me

Soon, I blossomed from the little girl with secrets into a young adult with open wounds. My best friend lived two doors up and my other closest friends lived right around the corner. The more I grew older, the unhappier I became. I started acting out because of all the pain that was brewing on the inside of me for all those years. I didn't have any outlet to express the pain. So, I used my behavior to channel my frustrations. I ran away from home numerous times. It felt good to be away from an unhappy, unsafe place. Oftentimes, I ran away to my best friend's house. Although she was only two houses up, my mother never thought to look there. Even when my mother called the house, my best friend lied and told her she hadn't seen me. Eventually, my mother got smart.

One day, she walked to my friend's house and asked for her mother. Of course, she told her that she could find me. Needless to say, they found me hiding in the basement. I had to come up with a new game plan of escape. I had another friend's house that I could go to where I knew my mother would never find me. This time, I was 15 houses away and on the other side of the street. I thought this was a better plan. It was a very small house and my friend's grandmother said she was not going to have any parts of me running away. After a while, my short-term escapes only led to long-term consequences. There was no escaping. There was no way to get away. I was being haunted and tormented from the inside out. I realized I was trying to escape something that I should have tried to confront instead. By this point, I was old enough to know that I should deal with the problems instead of trying to run away from them. When my mother got tired of looking for me and tired of chasing me, she called for help.

  She called my uncle, whom I really didn't talk to much. My uncle was stern in his speech and he never really thought about his actions. He didn't want anyone disrespecting his sisters—not even his nieces and nephews. My uncle didn't tolerate much nonsense. The last time that I decided to run away, I paid the price sooner than later. When I arrived back home, he had a gift for me. The gift was a four-inch, pure leather belt with a silver buckle. He told me to go outside, put my hands on the fence, and bend over. I didn't know what was coming. He hit me with the belt four times and it felt like I'd been hit a hundred times. This pain was a pain that went physically deeper than any other pain I'd ever felt. It went through my skin, warmed my blood and has now left physical scars on my body. Not only do I have the deep emotional pain, but I now have the deep physical pain to accompany it. I was trying to process how I felt but didn't know how.

I just knew I was hurting.

Pain became my new norm. I didn't expect anything, but rejection. The molestation, the abuse, the neglect, the abandonment, the rejection all took a toll on me. After I got what they called a whooping, but I call a beating, I decided to run away again. Despite the consequences, this time, I intended to be gone for a while.

Kidnapped and Raped

I found it amazing how the pain would lead into more pain—all because I'd never dealt with it. At some point, I was going to have to deal with the pain that was getting the best of me. Sometimes, we overlook things. We ignore things. But we rarely truly confront the pain. Even though pain is what I was running from, little did I know, it was what I kept running into. I didn't want to listen to my mother. When you are a teenager, you don't think your parents know best. I've learned that parents only do what they know. They can only give you what they are accustomed to having themselves. There's a price to pay that comes with rebellion and disobedience. We often don't realize what that price is until it's too late. When I ran away this time, it was my last time.

This time, I ran away to a family friend's house. I knew my mother would not find me there. I didn't know where he lived, but I thought I could trust him because he was so close to the family. He never gave me a reason not to trust him. After that beating I got from my uncle, I had to go. I called Kevin, who I had been friends with for years. He flirted with me here and there, but I never took him seriously. Kevin and my cousin always made fun of me and called me "Peck." How do you make fun of someone, but flirt with them at the same time? I asked him if I could come to his house after I ran away. I expressed to him that I didn't want my mother to find me.

When I arrived at his house, I thought about how much I was going to enjoy being away from home. I was finally about to have some space to clear my head. He didn't have much to eat, but I felt it was going to be a safe place. When I arrived, he was about to leave to go to work.

He came home from work later that night and it was like a different person walked through the door. I had never seen that person; I saw a side of him that I didn't know existed. When he got home, he became very demanding. Because he was doing me a favor, he felt entitled to something that wasn't his. I was about to be hit with the ultimate betrayal. He must have planned everything out before he'd left for work.

    He took out all the phone lines in his apartment. He made me strip down naked and made me take a bubble bath. Even though I told him I didn't want to take a bath, he told me I didn't have a choice. I went in the bathroom to bathe and shut the door behind me. I guess he heard me get into the tub, so he came in after me. He made me wash up in front of him, while he held an extension cord. As I was trying to cover up my body with my skinny hands and arms, I failed. My body was covered with bath bubbles—and the spirit of fear of the unknown.

    "I want to see the bubbles run down your body," he said.

As the bubbles ran down my body, tears ran down my face.

I was crying, begging him, "Please don't make me do this!"

With the extension cord in his hand, sitting on the toilet, he said, "Don't make me hit you with this cord. Now do what I told you to do," he said firmly.

This feeling had become all too painful. The violation was now all too common. What I thought I was running away from pushed me right into worse pain. There were no inside locks in the house. There was no way out. You could only get out the house with a key, and the door knob was on the outside of the door. Now, I was desperate to go back to the place that I once longed to escape from. The windows were walls. There was no way to communicate with the outside world. My only hope was to get ahold of the keys and unlock the door. The next night, he came home from work and wreaked havoc on me. He ordered me to go to the back room.

"No!" I told him. "For what?"

"You owe me some pussy and you're going to give it to me."

"I don't owe you anything! I'm ready to go home."

But he wouldn't let me go. He made me go to the back room and lie down on the nasty mattress. The sheet was only partially hanging onto the mattress. The mattress was almost black and heavily stained. The filth of the mattress seemed to represent nothing that I wanted to be associated with.

First, he told me, "Turn over on your stomach." Then, "Roll over."

I cried, begging and pleading with him, "Stop! Please stop! Please let me go home!"

He penetrated me over and over again. Tears flowed from me like they'd never flowed before. My virginity had now been taken away from me. It felt like he was never going to stop. The wounds ran so deep that I now had internal bleeding. No bandage could cover this wound. No amount of stitches could stop the bleeding. This day would replay in my mind. I was now mourning the death of what should have been a decision. This was not only traumatic to my body, but traumatic to my soul. I had lost something I could never get back. I was not only robbed of my childhood, I was robbed of my adulthood.

After the third day of being held hostage and being raped repeatedly, he decided to let me go home. I asked myself, *How many more secrets can a young child hold?* I didn't know what to do or who I could tell. Surely, no one would believe me. No one had believed me all my life. Why would they start believing me now? No one believed me about the molestation, so why would they believe me about the kidnapping and rape? I told one person who I thought would possibly believe me. Instead of believing me and listening to me, they bombarded me with questions. I held everything in. While I should have never ran away, I did not deserve what had happened to me. I was learning the true consequences of my actions. Life seemed to be all about instant self-gratification, no matter who got hurt in the process.

Becoming Independent

Even though I never told another soul, I was determined not to repeat my mistakes. After running away the last time, I decided I was going to live with my grandmother. I knew I needed to heal and deal with the hurt and pain. I needed to be somewhere I knew I would be loved and accepted. I had to be somewhere that I could process what I had been through, without going through any more pain. While staying with my grandmother, I was able to participate in extracurricular activities in school. I could just be *me*. While searching inside me, I was learning who I was. I had to study some of the things God had spoken to me. My grandmother was a very spiritual person. As long as I was in her house, I was going to serve the Lord. Being at her house allowed me to discover things about myself that I didn't know. It also allowed me to hear that inner voice that I would soon learn to know as the voice of God. I was growing at Grandma's house. I was slowly blossoming, but still needed to get rid of the weeds. I wanted something different, something new. How would Christeria take care of Christeria? While I didn't have the answer, I knew I would figure it out.

After staying with my grandmother for two years, I decided to live on my own. I went to apply for subsidized housing, which allowed me to pay only 30% of my income for rent. At the same time, it allowed me to become independent. I was working two jobs and also taking public transportation. I worked at U.S. Playing Cards during the day and Burger King at night. When I was off from my first job, I worked more hours at Burger King. One day, I got off work late and needed a ride home. I ran into Kevin and asked him if he could take me home. Years had gone by. So, when he asked me if he could come in, I thought nothing of it. He came in, sat on my blue floral couch, and started talking. I was exhausted from working two jobs. Independence was what I wanted, and it was what I got. While being on my own wasn't easy, the peace that came along with it was more than worth it.

While Kevin was sitting on the couch, I decided to go to my room and change clothes. I fell asleep from exhaustion though. In the middle of the night, I heard water running and saw a light seeping through the door. It felt as if I was dreaming because I was so exhausted. I lacked the energy to get up to see if something was going on or if I was truly dreaming. After waking up, I asked myself, *"What were you thinking to let him in your house? What was that dream all about?"* Two months had passed, and I was starting to feel extremely tired. This was a different kind of tired. I didn't have any energy. I had no desire to eat and I could no longer use my will power to push forward day by day.

One day, I had been asleep so long that I woke up and thought it was the next day. I had been asleep for 12 hours. I was still talking to Donnie, who I used to date when I was in high school. Donnie lived in Madisonville with his grandmother, and I lived in Avondale. I saw him from time to time because he was very active in sports. I was talking to Donnie one day and told him the way I was feeling. I'd also missed my period.

I went to the doctor's office and learned I was pregnant. I started spending the night more with Donnie at his grandmother's house, but we were not officially together. Donnie had left me in high school for another girl, but I still loved him. I hung out in Madisonville while he was at work. We were preparing for our baby girl to come into this world. After ten months of preparation, I was anxious for our baby girl to be born. Past the due date, and with my body running low on amniotic fluid, I was forced to deliver the baby. On July 29, 1994, she arrived into the world, healthy and with a full head of hair.

We enjoyed our new baby girl and learning how to be parents. While apart, we were learning to come together. I took my daughter around family and friends to show her off. I was so proud to be a mother. I dreamed about the future and what it held for me and baby girl. Traveling around the city, I often ran into Kevin. Ella, my baby girl, was three months when I ran into Kevin again.

Kevin immediately said, "That baby looks like me."

"The devil is a lie," I said.

I ran across Kevin again while he was with my cousin. He said it again.

"I'm telling you. That looks like my baby."

I said to him, "How could this possibly be your baby?"

He failed to answer. I knew it had been years since he had raped me. There was no way that I could birth a baby from years ago. I was trying to process what he was saying and, most importantly, figure out why he was saying what he was saying.

Kevin said, "Take the baby to my mama."

"Why would I do that?"

He said, "Just take the baby to my mama and I will show you."

I told Donnie about the craziness of what was being said, and he asked himself the same questions. I knew I had nothing to hide. Just so we could shut him up, I took Ella to Martha, his mother.

She said, "Yep, that is my granddaughter."

"No way. How could you say that and how do you know?" I asked.

She said, "Look at her feet. Everyone in my family has those feet and I recognize my baby by her feet."

The bigger question I was asking myself was, "How?" I told Donnie what Kevin's mother said. I also explained to Donnie that I had no clue what he or she was talking about. I didn't know what his mother was seeing. I had to remember who I was dealing with.

So, I asked Donnie, "What do you think? Should we take the DNA test?"

Donnie said, "Take the test to get him off your back."

I went to the Department of Job and Family Services for the DNA test. Surprisingly, the test came back 99.98% that Kevin was indeed the father. I was completely appalled with the results! I knew in my heart of hearts that this could not be. I was in tears. I was hurt. I was in pain. I was disappointed, and I had so many unanswered questions. *Why is this happening?*

How could this be? When did this happen? Why don't I remember anything? This seems so surreal.

I cried uncontrollably. While Donnie and I weren't together, I felt like he would be a better father than Kevin could ever be. I didn't want my daughter to have the DNA of a kidnapper and rapist, the DNA of an abuser and a liar. I now had a child with a man who repeatedly raped me, but I didn't know how. I knew I would never put myself in a position to be violated like that again.

But I had. The night I had fell asleep and left Kevin on my couch, I woke up feeling like I was in a dream. But I didn't know if I was dreaming or not. I blamed myself. I was ashamed. I was dying inside for help. While Kevin never gave me an answer about how our daughter was conceived, I soon learned the answer. Five years after our daughter was born, I heard and confirmed that he was convicted of statutory rape and corruption of a minor. While I would never get justice on the wounds he created, and what he stole from me, I'm was elated on my behalf that someone else did.

3

Hoping for a New Life

At the age of 20, life started to take a turn for the better. Still dealing with the hurts, wounds, issues, pains and challenges of the past, I continuously pressed forward to my future. I was not giving up hope. I was not giving up on all the dreams that I had as a little girl. I couldn't shake those dreams that God showed me when I was a child, but never talked about. I've always dreamed of having and obtaining everything in life as an adult that I missed as a child. I always dreamed of feeling loved, accepted and protected. I dreamed of having someone fight for me versus someone violating me. I dreamed of creating the life that I always envisioned.

My life was taking a turn for the better and I was in love. Although I was in love, I realized I still had issues and pain that I needed to deal with. While most of my wounds were created out of broken trust, other wounds were created from my poor choices and bad decisions. It was important to me that the relationship that I was about to enter worked because everything else in my life didn't. I couldn't afford another disappointment to enter my heart, which was already so fragile. How do you deal with issues you've never addressed internally? How do I die to the old and embrace the new? How do I not contaminate a new relationship with old waste that I've yet to get rid of?

Marcus and I crossed paths some time ago at Eden Park. We exchanged telephone numbers and conversed on a daily basis. With all that I had been through, I didn't want to set myself up to fail. So, I knew I had to do something different. I was now a single mother with a beautiful baby girl. Our relationship started off slow, but it was serious. There was no immediate intimacy and there was a lot of delayed gratification. While we didn't jump right into a relationship, we did jump right into our dreams, goals and aspirations. He was going to college out of state, and I attended college in-state. After a year, we became intimate and our relationship began to flourish. With all the wrongs that had happened in my life, I finally felt like I was doing something right. I was finally on the right path. Ella's father and I talked here and there, but there was no consistency in his effort to have a relationship with his child. Although she may have been too young to know what was going on, she was never too young to be loved and embraced. I wanted her to have what I never had. This long-distance relationship was okay for a season, but I wanted more. I stopped going to college because I really didn't know what I wanted to do with my life.

My daughter Ella and I moved to Tennessee. Marcus attended school by day, and I worked at night. After living in Tennessee for several years, Marcus graduated from Tennessee State University and we moved back to Cincinnati, Ohio, where we were both born and raised. After five years of dating, we decided that we were going to get married. Wanting more out of life, and putting my all into my marriage, we made the joint decision to move away. With only $1100 in savings, first month's rent paid, but no jobs lined up for either of us, we decided to take a leap of faith. We had different levels of faith, which led to different levels of actions. The one thing that I remember about the God I would hear so much about was that the only thing that pleases Him is Faith. We leaped by Faith.

We packed up our entire family and moved to Atlanta. By this time, I had two children. On November 7, 1998, I birthed another beautiful baby girl. It was a complicated pregnancy, both emotionally and physically. Marcus and I had lost our first baby to a miscarriage earlier that year. I remember the vivid images of learning that I was pregnant, but then shortly seeing the fetus come out in the toilet. I learned that everything happens for a reason. I rejoiced in the fact we had a healthy baby girl now. We moved and got settled in. Now, it was time to trust God.

    This was a God move, not just a good move. God spoke to me clearly right before we made the decision to move. A week after moving, Marcus found a job and he received a large sign on bonus, working for the bank. Sometimes, it's faith that brings us to our destiny and faith that helps us stay there. You have to believe in what you are praying for. Through everything that happened to me, I learned how to build a relationship with God. I went to church even more, even though it was just me and the children. While Marcus was working, I was a stay-at-home mom, learning how to fix credit. After his first paycheck, he mistakenly received another signing bonus. He immediately informed the bank about it and they told him he could keep it. Life was good! This fresh start that we desired was getting better by the day.

Shortly after we moved, I sat in the house and learned how to fix credit because we wanted to purchase a home. I fixed Marcus' credit and we purchased our first home approximately six months after moving to Georgia. We built it from the ground up and picked out every last detail of the interior. Life was extraordinarily good. I was getting everything I financially and physically wanted in life. But emotionally, I was starving. I believe my emotional starvation came from my lack of a father. I had wounds that hadn't healed. We had a brand-new home, built from the ground up. Marcus secured me a job at the bank, and I was working part-time, only seven minutes away from our home. My spirit was still telling me something wasn't right, but I didn't quite know what it was.

My gift of prophecy mostly comes to me through dreams. One day, I was sitting on the couch and God spoke to me. He said, "You're about to go through a storm." God's voice was loud and clear. I questioned if it was the voice of God because, at the time, everything seemed to be going just fine. Seven days to the day, the U.S. Marshalls knocked at the door. They were looking for my husband, Marcus. Little did I know, Marcus was caught up in a check fraud ring that consisted of 28 people from Georgia to Florida. At the time,

Marcus was the branch manager at the bank. Turns out, he was giving his best friend bank account numbers. I could clearly see the storm; however, I don't believe that it was meant to be destructive. What this storm did was clear the path for me to birth what was deep down inside of me. The one thing I learned about my unhealed hurts was that I was constantly looking for what I knew I had within, in others. After I learned what was going on, I knew I had to do something else and make changes in my life.

Desperate for Change

After learning what Marcus had done, I knew the odds were against me and my family. I had to make some immediate decisions. I took a new position at the bank, but now, I was further away from home. We were now living in West Marietta, Georgia, and the new position was in Norcross, Georgia. With the Feds on my husband's back and U.S. Marshalls monitoring us, once again, I felt so betrayed. I asked myself, and him, the hard questions. *How could a man, who said he loved his wife and family, set himself up to possibly be away from them?* All of my questions would be answered with time, but no answer would take away the pain and betrayal I felt.

When I met Marcus, I was a single mother. But I didn't have intentions on going back to being one. Still pursuing my marriage, the day to face the judge came. Marcus was sentenced to twelve months and one day to federal boot camp in Atlanta. While Marcus accepted the plea deal, with good behavior, he would serve ten months in federal boot camp. That was the exact time he served, and it seemed like eternity. The kids and I visited Marcus every Sunday after church. I snuck food in for Marcus, praying I would never get caught. They randomly picked people to search to make sure they weren't bringing outside items into the camp. People would sneak cell phones, money and drugs in. You name it, the women brought it in. I saw them pull whole containers out of their brassieres. The men at the camp had prostitutes come in the camp to have sex with them at night. Marcus would sneak on the phone to call me and he would beg me to bring him a phone. I never did because, if he got caught with a phone, he would get more time. I was not about to be responsible for Marcus getting more time on my account. I told him to continue to use the phones that were available to him.

One day while visiting Marcus and sitting at the table, he and I had a candid conversation. He asked me some questions that came with hard answers. One of the questions he yielded my candid response, "I only stayed with you because of the children." When I made that comment, Marcus said that he wanted a divorce. He should have never said that. After all I'd been through, I didn't want anyone who didn't want me. The entire time I was married to him, I wanted so much out of life. I was constantly asking him to start a business. He always agreed, but never moved on the idea. It wasn't until Marcus went away that I realized the entire time I was trying to get Marcus to become something, God was telling me to become an entrepreneur. Our marriage wasn't bad; it was actually a pretty good marriage. I was just emotionally deprived. Marcus was a yes-man. While I thought I wanted a yes-man, his yes was mere deprivation of all the times he told me, "No" that lied on the inside of me. Internalizing all that was happening, all that had happened, I was desperate for change. I was desperate to provide for my family.

My vision became clearer. I heard the voice of God more. Not only did I see His hand, but I understood more how

God's hand was moving in my life. After relocating to a high-profile branch in Norcross, Georgia, and signing a confidentiality agreement, I learned that you often have to become comfortable in the uncomfortable places. Desperate for change and looking for answers, a lady came to the bank who was depositing a $9,000 real estate check. Two days later, the same lady came into my branch twice in the same day and deposited two more checks. One of the checks was a little over $8,000; the other check was close to $9,000. I had literally just watched a lady make almost $27,000 in three days. That was it. I was going to real estate school to become a real estate agent. Working for the bank, I lacked the funds needed to go to real estate school. However, I took another leap of faith. I wrote a check that I didn't have the funds to cover. I wrote three separate checks for $160 each and they all cleared on time. After studying and successfully passing my real estate test the third time, it was time to make some real money.

 All the ladies at my branch asked me if I could help them purchase a home. Forced with an ultimatum from the branch manager, I had to make another life decision. The branch manager told me that having a real estate license was a conflict of interest. I had to now make a decision to stay at the bank or give up the real estate license that I had worked so hard to get.

"God, what say you?" I asked.

God said, "I've never let you down before and I am not going to start now. Trust me."

So, that's what I did. I told Ann, the branch manager, that I would be keeping my real estate license and turning in my resignation. I went home and typed up my resignation letter, prayed about it, and turned it in the next day. Toward the end of the day, the branch manager and the business banker came to me and said, "They accepted your resignation. You're eligible for rehire, but today is your last day. You will get paid for two weeks, even with you leaving today." What a mighty God we serve! God is better than good. Mind you, when I turned in that resignation, I had $125.32 in the bank and no backup plan. However, I made $11,500 the first 30 days in commission! That was almost my entire salary of $18 an hour a week for working at the bank. Again, you can't tell me what my God won't do. An entrepreneur was birthed.

I was rocking and rolling with my real estate license and enjoying my newfound success. I had actually found something I loved to do, and I was able to help people in the process. I went from making $12,100 a year to now $7,000 to $15,000 a month. I had to find my niche. I knew I was different and I wanted to do something different. So I became the bad credit queen. I fixed customers' credit and turned them into clients before I helped them purchase a new home. I placed signs on the corner that told people I could help them get into a home, even with bad credit. One guy who started off as a client is now a good friend. He had a 499-credit score and purchased his first home with that 499-credit score. He purchased a home in Kennesaw, Georgia and received a 7.35% fixed 30-year interest rate. To this day, he still owns that house. His credit score had risen to almost 800 now, and he's ready to purchase another home. Moving and shaking in the real estate game, I was anxious to learn more.

    I was obtaining more, and, by this time, I had my third child. She went to most of my real estate closings with me. She was born on October 3, 2006. I had switched brokers quite a few times, trying to learn all I could learn about this real estate game. Each real estate broker had something different to offer. One of the last real estate brokers I was with changed the game for me. He was young, black and had six different locations. After being in business a short period of time, he had almost 400 agents under his agency. He had to make at least $4 million a year. Well, he confirmed some of my assumptions about his revenue for his agency. The more I learned in the game, the more I earned. A year and a half after being newly licensed, I qualified to become a broker. I had met the sales goal and the number of transactions that was required to have my own agency. The key was I had to wait until my two-year anniversary to actually get my real estate broker's license. The new entrepreneur was birthed.

    I opened my own real estate brokerage and had approximately 10 agents under my belt over the course of my life as a real estate broker. Life was good. Money was good, and business was good. Little did I know that it wouldn't be good for long. In 2007, the economic recession hit, and my life took a drastic turn. I lost over 40 subprime lenders in one day. I was just faced with a possible divorce and now, a recession. Again, my mind started asking, *Why me? There has to be something better in store.* I'd had three blows in one week, and it felt like I was about to hit rock bottom. My entire niche was being laid to rest. I no longer had lending companies to service my targeted audience. I had done so well with people who other real estate agents often overlooked. I had done so well for the people who were often rejected because their credit was less than perfect. This became my niche. I could easily identify with what it felt like to be overlooked. I knew the pain associated with not being accepted.

It's hard to help someone through something that you haven't experienced personally. I learned to monetize on my pain through real estate sales. I didn't know it at the time I was working to fix my ex-husband's credit, but God knew it would serve a greater purpose down the line. I didn't mind taking the time out to genuinely help people because, for decades, I screamed for help. However, no one would listen to me. Helping people became second nature for me. It's what I often longed for, but never received.

While the recession had hit, and my marriage was on the rocks, I was still battling in my mind. *Do I save my marriage or let it go? Do I find a new niche, or do I give up?* Because I was so broken, and never took the time to heal, I believe I made irrational decisions. I walked away from a marriage, from a person, who was good to me. However, he was not necessarily the one for me. I have no regrets. I decided not to get a new niche, but to just stop doing real estate.

I needed a break. I needed a breather. A person can only take so many losses at once. I was at my peak. I didn't want another loss, but some things happen that you can't control. I dealt with the losses as they came. I tried to turn every loss into an opportunity to grow in some way, shape, form or fashion. However, I didn't know how to recover from the losses. I didn't have a Plan B. After hearing the voice of God, after much prayer and thought, I decided to go back home.

    I made that decision after my house was struck by lightning. Not only was I practically losing it, but I was running out of savings. Once again, I had to make decisions that were best for survival and my emotional stability. I packed and prepared to go home. By this time, I had four children. I gave birth to a beautiful baby boy on January 28, 2008.

4

Beaten and Broken

After living in Atlanta for almost ten years, it was time to return to Cincinnati. I'd exhausted all resources, and I was broke and still broken. I knew there was hope, but there always will be if you can just see yourself outside of your current situation. I moved back home October 30, 2009 and settled into my mother's home. Immediately, I felt sad and depressed about the lack of options that I had to relocate. A week after being home, I started looking for a new church home. I was invited to attend a friend's church in suburbs of Cincinnati, Ohio. Church was good that day, but I knew that wouldn't be the church for me.

After church was over, I was standing in the vestibule waiting on my friend. While standing in the vestibule, I was approached by a gentleman who introduced himself, but failed to use his name. A minute later, my friend Ralph came out to the vestibule and thanked me for coming. He invited me out to Dave & Buster's to celebrate his cousin's birthday. I went to the birthday celebration later that evening and, surprisingly, the guy who was talking to me in the vestibule was there as well. He continued the conversation that he'd started at the church. We exchanged telephone numbers and chatted for three hours that night. We discussed our backgrounds, our children, our occupations and some family history. It appeared as if we had a lot in common. It seemed like we had some of the same goals.

However, the relationship went faster than the speed of light. We became intimate after only three weeks of dating and he immediately introduced the concept of marriage. This was new to me. I really didn't know how to process someone asking me to marry them after such a short period of time. Because I was so broken, I felt like it was love. Even though I had second thoughts, I ignored them. Because I had some business to tend to in Georgia, Tommy and I took a quick trip. I wanted him to meet my good friend, Ricky. Ricky was the gentleman who helped me understand that I had the gift of prophecy. I could call Ricky if I needed clarity on anything. Ricky was right 99.7% of the time. Tommy met Ricky, and Ricky drilled Tommy as if Ricky was my biological brother. After we returned to Ohio, Ricky called me and said that he didn't think Tommy was good for me.

"How do you know?" I asked him.

"Because he wouldn't look me straight in the eyes," Ricky said. "Any time a man won't look you straight in the eyes, he has something to hide."

I chose to overlook Ricky's concern. I really wanted to get out of my mother's house. I wanted my independency back. I'd been on my own since I was 18 years old. So living with someone else, including my mother, at the age of 32 made me feel like less of a woman.

A couple of months later, Tommy and I decided that we were so much in love that we didn't want to continue living in sin by having sex. We decided to get a place together. Tommy knew that I wanted to move into an area that had a decent school district because I wanted to get my children back. I had left my oldest two children in Georgia with their dad because I wanted to make sure they remained stable. We started looking at apartments in West Chester, Ohio. We found a two-bedroom apartment that was in our budget. We moved in January 22, 2010, a little less than two months of us meeting each other. Things were good. We were in love and we were working to build a future together.

We decided we were going to get married soon. On a bright sunny day in February 2010, we decided that was going to be our day. It was the day that we had known each other exactly three months. When I woke up that morning, I didn't feel my best. After an hour, I noticed that I had the pink eye in both eyes. One eye was worse than the other, so I could barely see. Both of my eyes were swollen. I called one of my high school girlfriends, Kayla, to get her spiritual opinion of what was going on.

"Your sight is being blinded," Kayla said. "Maybe God is trying to tell you not to get married. You are not seeing straight. Maybe it's a sign not to get married."

Well, I got married with two pink eyes. I thought we would live happily ever after. But, deep in my heart, I felt something was wrong. I just didn't know what. A few family members, and his pastor friend who was going to marry us, came to the wedding. Now, we were happily married. Things were good. I had found a job at an insurance company and I was still working on real estate deals in Georgia from

Cincinnati. One day, I got a random call from my child's father, Kevin. Kevin told me that my now husband was talking to a chick named Gwen from Madisonville. He said she was a cute girl and she had a big butt. I asked Tommy about this and he denied it, of course. Tommy snatched the phone from me and told me how he was going to beat Kevin's behind. Tommy said he didn't know the girl and he didn't know anything about her. Kevin reassured me that it was the truth because it was one of the women that he was still pimping. I listened to what Tommy was saying. But, deep down inside, I didn't believe a thing he was telling me. I started praying about the entire situation.

One day, he left to go to work. My daughter and my son were in the house playing. I guess in the midst of them playing, they found a cell phone. I turned the cell phone on. Not only was Gwen's name in the phone, but her mother's telephone number was in the phone as well. This was the start of what was about to come. Some time passed, and things were going fairly well. I had not talked to Kevin because Tommy had asked me to respect our marriage and not talk to him. One late night in April of 2010, I called Tommy's cell phone. However, he didn't answer. Tommy worked second shift at the time. Something didn't feel right about this situation. Because we shared a phone bill, we both had access to each other's cell phone records. My spirit told me something wasn't right. I logged into our online cell phone account to see if he was on the phone when I was calling. Sure enough, he was on the phone talking to Latonya. I blocked my number and called the telephone number on the phone bill. I got a voicemail but, she said her name was Latonya on her recording.

By the time Tommy arrived at the house, I had taken the mattress and made a spot in the living room on the floor because I was studying. I didn't want to disturb him because I knew he would be tired when he got off work. Tommy walked through the door and I asked to see his phone. He gave me his phone.

"I was calling you and you didn't answer," I said. He gave me some lame excuse, not knowing that I had looked at the phone bill already. I looked at his phone and the number was no longer there.

"What happened to the Latonya's telephone number? You deleted it?" I asked

"I don't know what you are talking about!"

"Well, I do. See! Look. When you didn't answer my phone call, I looked on the phone bill. Here her number is."

In a split second, he snapped. He picked me up, slammed me on the mattress, threw me up against the wall and he tried to throw me out of the second-floor window. I was trying to get away, so he grabbed me and scratched up my arm. He kept slamming me onto the mattress. Then, I ran into the bedroom. I knew he was obsessed with his clothes. So, I went to the closet and took all of his clothes out. I threw them on the floor in an attempt to make him stop. I thought he would be more worried about the clothes than about me. He picked up the phone and said he was going to call the police and tell them *I'd hit him*. And he did just that. Three minutes later, I heard sirens.

West Chester Police came and Tommy told a blatant lie. He told the police that I put my hands on him because I found out that he was talking to a female. The cops got both sides of the story and determined that he was the abuser. They arrested him and locked him up that night on the spot. I was so heartbroken. *How could this be? What did I do to deserve this?* This seemed like the same question I had been asking myself for decades. He went to jail that night and all I could do was cry myself to sleep. The memories of when I had pink eye in both eyes, and how God was really trying to warn me about what I was about to get myself into all came back to me. I should have listened and paid attention to the warning signs. My life was forever changed—*again*.

Tommy got out of jail a couple days later. The judge ordered him to take anger management classes. He promised he would change and that he'd never do it again.
I believed him. I didn't want to give up on my marriage, so I kept going. Well, it wasn't long before things escalated and got worse. I sought private help and couldn't get it. No one would listen. I was even told to be careful about who I spoke to about our problems because it seemed like I was spreading rumors and trying to defame him. I had no voice. I had no options. And I had little to no one to talk to about my problems. Being married to a prominent pastor's son was not easy. It came with a whole lot of wolves in sheep's clothing.

One pastor and his wife always listened to me and always helped me and the children out. They bought us food, listened to me cry, and offered any kind of assistance that we needed. I felt so bad. I never wanted to expose my children to this, but I did. I wanted a voice, but I had none. I felt like I was stuck in a relationship that I was never going to get out of. I lived in West Chester and I had no form of transportation. The vehicle was in his name, which he took often and left me in the house. When I really wanted out, I called numerous shelters. However, none of them offered transportation services. I was *stuck*. I never wanted my children to live this life. I always wanted to give my children a better life than what I had growing up. I was failing my children *and myself.*

    I was so fragile, physically and emotionally. I'd been thrown into a brick wall. I was almost thrown out of a window. I was pushed out of a moving vehicle at 25 miles per hour on Mulhauser Road. He grabbed my arms so tight that he always left bruises that were imprints of his fingerprints. He took my purse so I couldn't start work. He threw me into a baby bouncer when I was pregnant and he broke the entire bouncer. The abuse was so bad that I became a zombie until I knew it was safe to get away. That day, I loaded my car, called my mother and left. I had to get out of that house. I had enough of the abuse. I was so scared to leave and uproot my children from their environment.

    I was worried about what he would do to me when he found out that I was really gone. I went to the leasing office and explained to them what was going on. I begged them to help me because I knew I couldn't stay with my mother forever because the children had to go to school. The apartment complex had a rule that if the police were called on multiple occasions, they had a right to do a voluntary eviction. Sure enough, they called us into the office and explained to us that we had to go.

One of us could stay, but not both of us. They helped me get him out of the house. I knew there was one more thing that we had to do, though. I had missed my period. The signs were all there that I was pregnant. I told him before he left for good that he had to go to the doctor's office with me to see if I was pregnant. The doctor only confirmed what I already knew to be true. I was so sad. I was about to have another baby with a man who I did not love. I couldn't even stand to look at him.

After we came from the doctor's office, he dropped me off. I called the front office and told them to change the locks. They waived the fee for me. I didn't have any form of transportation. With a house full of five children, I could never figure out why no one told him to give me the vehicle. We were surrounded by so many Christians. After all, his parents were pastors. He took the car and hid it at his parents' house.

The finance company called me because they wanted to repossess it, but they couldn't get in the gate to his parents' home.

I spoke to my sister on the phone and told her that he had taken the car. She just so happened to be talking to her baby's daddy, Paul, who brought me an old car. It was January 21, 2012. I remember that day like it was yesterday. On that day, I also had to renew my lease with no job and no income. We had never been late on our rent, so they automatically renewed my lease. I heard the voice of God so clearly.

God said, "You are going to have to trust me like you never trusted me before."

And that I did. Rick Warren said, "You never know God is all you need until God is all you got."

I didn't have anything or anyone else, except for God at this point. As I started putting my belongings in the car, Tommy drove past.

He yelled, "So now you want to get a car? Why couldn't you get a car when we were together?" The car Paul gave me had challenges. Paul gave me the title to the car and told me I could do whatever I needed to do with the vehicle. So, I took the vehicle and traded it in. I went on Dixie Highway and found a little purple 1997 Toyota Corolla. With five children and one on the way, a vehicle with only five seats wasn't big enough. I had a close friend who helped transport me and my children when I had places to go. She went out of her way to make sure all of my children rode in the car safely. She also made sure we had something to eat.

As the days went on, Tommy became very irrational. For some reason, he would not accept that we were not going to be together. He started stalking me. I went to court to get a restraining order after he kept calling my phone and threatening to kill me. At first, the court gave me a temporary restraining order. Then, we had a hearing and they issued a permanent restraining order for five years. There was no way to describe the way I felt about the decisions I made during the course of my life. I wanted to heal so badly. It all seemed like a bad nightmare. I just wanted it all to go away. Ten months later, on October 30, 2012, I birthed my sixth and last child.

5

Letters of the Broken Hearted

I had been through so much in life at this point that I was simply trying to process it all.
I was trying to process why one person has to go through so much. I thought about how unfair life can truly be. We often don't ask for the things we get, but we get the things subconsciously we often want. Some things cannot be prevented, and we cannot change the hand of time. Some children get molested, while other children get praised. I never understood why God hated me so much that He let such horrific things happen to me. I always knew there was a God. I often praised the God I grew to know.

Feeling rejected by my mother, abandoned by my father, raped by my stepfather, kidnapped and raped by who I thought was my friend and beaten by my husband, I'd endured more than most endure in a lifetime. After a while, it was hard not to expect every victory to be followed by a disappointment. I started crying out to God. I started building a better relationship with God, but it wasn't perfect. I was being real with God, but not necessarily real with myself. I often looked at the wounds I had, but not the self-inflicted cuts that were the precursors to opening them. I decided one day I was going to divorce the devil. I was going to cry and write until God could hear me, until I could feel the shift in my life. I grew to understand that everything doesn't happen when we want it to, but it usually happens right on time.

Dear Devil,

> I am writing this letter to tell you that I no longer want to be your girlfriend. I know we have a long history together, and we have had an on-and-off relationship for quite some time now. But it is finally time to say, "Goodbye." I have a new man in my life, and His name is Jesus. Devil, I know when we were together, we had a lot of good times and some bad times. Although I thought our time together was good, you were not who you made yourself out to be. You made me think that my vision was clear, but it was really blurry. See, you made me believe that clubbing, gambling, drinking, gossiping and being disobedient was all good behavior. The men were handsome, and some even

gorgeous. The sex was off the chain and, most of the time, amazing. Devil, I never questioned our loyalty because everything looked and felt so good while I was doing it.

July 26, 2011 8:42 AM

Dear God,

I cannot seem to understand, for the life of me, all the things that have transpired in my life. Ever since I was nine years old, I knew that you made me different. I seem to be in this new place. This place of discomfort, misunderstanding, hindrances, adversity and opposition. It seems like everyone is attacking me and everything is coming against me. I am trying to get my fight back, but I just don't know where to start at times. I feel like the devil has a hold of my brain. I am in this place where I feel like I am never going to be successful, never going to have anything, never going to become anyone. I know I was not just born to die. I was born with a purpose. I know God has given me the power to obtain riches and wealth, but where is it? Why does it seem like every time I try to exercise my faith, nothing happens? What is it about me that makes you forget about me?

I am a mother with five children, and I want to be the very best role model that I can be for them. I do not want my children looking at me as if I am a failure. I want my children to know and see that I did all I could do for them. It seems like I used to be on top of the world. But now, I am at rock bottom. You know Rick Warren states, "You never know God is all you need until God is all you have." I believe that statement to be so true, but the problem is you're not showing up. I'm thankful for my good health and all the blessings that you have bestowed upon me and my family, but I constantly ask myself, "Why me?" At first, I thought I had the answer. Now, I just don't know. I was fighting to get to this place, which I'm not even sure I belong to anymore. I want to be someone. I want to go somewhere. I have been going through for so long and it seems like everyone wins, but me. All these people doing all the wrong things, and I try to always do what's right. It seems as if everyone wins, but me.

You know about ten years ago, you placed it in my spirit that I was the next big thing. I believe that with all my heart and soul. No one could tell me anything different. I just don't know what to believe. It seems like I am just fighting to get my hope back. I have been through so much within the last two years that I have lost track of all that I have been through. I gave up my real estate company. All my precious belongings were put out on the street. All of my commercial deals fell through. My crazy children's father ran me out of Georgia. I find myself ultimately being in this place where I never wanted to be.

Ohio wasn't the place where I was used to seeing people thriving. The opportunities are limited, and success seems to be far and in between. I find myself in a physically abusive relationship. I find myself surrounded by a whole bunch of people who call themselves Christians, but don't have a clue about Christianity. They judge me. They persecute me, and they put me down. They condemn me. They talk about me. They're fake with me. The sad part about all of it is that none of them even know me. I find myself pregnant with my sixth child and can't even stand alone on my own two feet. I've endured so much pain, and so many heartaches and disappointments. People always talk about how talented I am, but no one ever acts like it. I can't even finance the panties I have on because my credit is so bad. I don't know where to begin, who to turn to and what to do. I turn to you, God, but you don't seem to be there. I turn to the people I know, but many of them have the same problems I do.

God, I just don't know what to do. God, I need you now more than I ever needed you in my life! Why did you leave me, God? I feel a sense of abandonment. My father left me. My mother really never cared for me. All the men in my life have hurt me. I thought things would be different when I got to a certain point in my life. I feel like I have disappointed myself to the point that there is no turning back or getting up. How does a woman, who doesn't have a pot to piss in, prevail? How do I heal all the unhealed hurts and pains, all the disappointments? How do I forgive all those who have persecuted me? I want so much more for me and my family. I just want you to show up and be God. I want a supernatural blessing, a supernatural breakthrough. I want to know that it was God, and God alone, that came through for me.

I have no money, no food, no car, no assets, and a ton of liabilities. No one will hire me. They say I'm overqualified. I have all these babies' daddies and none of them will support their children. There is no reason for me to be in the place that I am in. But I just can't seem to get out of it. I have been raped, molested, tied up and beat with extension cords. I've been locked in the house with no way out. I've been stuck in this little, old apartment with seven people and we only have three bedrooms. I know that I am capable of more. I know that I am a natural born leader, but somehow and some way, I got lost in the wilderness. Is this the plan you have for me, or is this the consequence for a host of bad decisions that I've made?

I never thought that I would come to this place in my life. I thought I had all the questions and the answers. I thought that I had a plan. I thought you would back me up on the plans that I had for my life. But when you didn't show up, and when you didn't appear like you've shown up in the past three years, I started to question my faith. I know you're with me, but I don't feel you. I don't see you. I don't see your face. At times, I just don't know how we made it or survived.

August 8, 2011 11:30 AM

Dear God,

God, things are not going nearly as I want them to go. Here I go again, feeling like I'm in this place of failure. I just want to get out of this marriage, but I don't want to feel like I failed again. There are so many people out there who want my marriage to fail. At the same time, I do not want it to work. The only thing that holds me is the fact that I just want to prove them wrong. But, trying to prove people wrong, and dealing with all of this abuse, has taken a toll on me. My husband is very abusive to me and it's only a matter of time before he really hurts me. I have made up in my mind that I have to walk away from this marriage. I have so many tears to shed, but don't know how to shed them. I'm in so much distress, yet I don't know where to begin. I am trying to get rid of these unmet needs, unhealed hurts and unresolved issues. Don't know how, don't know when and I don't know where. What I do know is that they have to go. It's keeping me from walking in all that God has for me. It's hindering me from all the blessings that God has in store for me. It's stopping me from operating and walking in pure love. My prayer is that God will heal and mend my heart.

The Bible says that God will never put more on you than you can handle. I do not believe that to be true. There is way too much on me. I have to deal with some of these hardcore issues that I am having. They're really getting to me. I do not know how to deal with them.
I am so unhappy in the place that I am, and the only person who can change that is me. I'm broke, busted and disgusted right now. I'm tired and I'm fed up with all this chaos and all of this drama. Whew... I do not know what I married into, but it is a mess. I am not willing to sit back and let people keep doing the things they have been doing to me.

I hate my life! Only I can change it! I hate what I have become and what I married into! This is not me and I'm going to get myself back, even if I have to walk away from everything that appears to be keeping me (but not). If it takes all that I have, it's worth it.

August 12, 2011 7:11:29 PM

Dear God,

Whew...I can't believe I made it through this day! My life sucks and I am really, really praying to get this job. This seems like an excellent opportunity to get some financial stability in my life. I have been without a stable income since 2007. It has been four long years. It has been two years since I had a car and, whew! I just don't know how I have survived so long with five children and no vehicle. I'm ready to climb to the top of the ladder, but I just don't know what ladder to get on. I have all these dreams and goals of being successful and all of these visions of me being such a renowned person. But I see no opening, no outlet, to everything that lies inside of me.

Why me? This saga continues. My heart hurts. I don't know how to deal with so much pain and adversity. I keep praying that you'll get me out of this situation, but it just seems like you've forgotten about me. I am trying to master this thing they call forgiveness. How do you forgive someone who has hurt you so bad? How do you forgive someone who has done you wrong over and over again?

How do you heal from all the pain, let it go and move on? Lord, how do you let it go? Why does it seem like I am so loyal, but people always disappoint me? While I live in this small city, people here have a problem with keeping their word. I'm just so discouraged and confused. I just don't know where to pick up. I trust you, Lord. I honor you, Lord, and I know that you are you. But where are you? Where have you been? Why haven't you shown up for me? Why do I feel like you have abandoned me? Why have you allowed me to get in this horrible situation? Why have you allowed me to marry into this?

As I lay in the bed and think about ways to take my life, I wonder if I shall go on or not. What has brought me to this point? The struggle is too great. The stress is too much and the pain is too deep. Where did I lose control? Why does it seem like I lose all of my battles? I'm trying to get my fight back. I'm trying to get my fight back! But, right now, I don't have enough strength to even get in the ring.

August 19, 2011 1:32:05 AM

Dear God,

 As I sit here and lay in my bed, I constantly ask myself, "Why me?" It seems like I have all of these hopes and dreams to do big things. I have hopes and dreams to become somebody one day. While I have been through a bit much over the last couple of weeks, that divorce is knocking at my door. I constantly ask myself, "Why did you get married so fast? Who are you really married to?" I don't seem to know anymore. I feel like I never knew in the first place. Why is my husband so abusive? Why does my husband feel like every time he gets mad, he can put his hands on me? I can't sit back and let people treat me this way. All my life, I feel like I have been abused, neglected, set aside and never accepted. I do not know why people have a problem accepting me because I call myself being real and authentic. Is it that people cannot really handle the truth, or people can't deal with the fact that I don't tolerate BS? Every night when I go to bed, I dream of a way to get out of this thing called marriage. I dream of ways to tell everyone off who has hurt me.

I can't believe this woman had the audacity to call me and tell me that my husband and I were not godly because we don't come around. Why would we come around them? They never have anything nice to say and they always think that they are right. I sit back and play a flashback over my life. I don't know what to think of it. I am 36 years old. My account is in the negative $600. I have no money to buy my children school clothes and supplies. I have no car to call my own. I have nothing. I repeat, *nothing*. I feel like everything has been stripped away. Everyone around me prevails, except for me. I know God has called me to do this thing, but I am starting to wonder if I have the right calling. Why don't people understand me? Why don't they listen to me and hear my heart? Why do they seem to misunderstand me? Why do they seem to misconstrue the things that I am not saying for the things that they would like to hear? Is life that complicated?

I am surrounded by so many people who don't look like me. No one can relate to what I am going through and what I have been through. It seems like I have no direction in life anymore. I just cannot accept sitting back and waiting to die one day, without leaving a legacy for my children. I feel like people overlook my greatness and my talents because I'm broke, busted and disgusted. I don't think people see me for who I really am. I know who you have called me to be, God. God, I am asking that you use me.

August 26, 2011 10:58 PM

Dear God,

Wow! It has been a long journey and it seems like nothing is getting better. This morning, our washer and dryer broke. Tuesday, August 23, they cut our cell phones off. It seems like life is getting harder. It's getting very hard to survive at this point. I have been waiting almost one month for a job at Prudential and one and a half weeks for a job at U.S. Bank. Nothing is coming through. So, we have no gas money. We have no money for diapers. The baby has no baby wipes. I just don't know what to do. I thought I was at my lowest. I guess not.

March 18, 2014

What do you do when you feel like the weight of the world is on your shoulders? Why did you entrust me with so many lives, but little means to take care of them? Why does it seem like I'm always fighting a battle? The Bible says the battle is not mine, it's the Lord's. Why does it seem like I've been fighting and trying to get this thing called success, but I can never achieve it? Why did you place so much in me, yet my dreams still go unfulfilled? Why have you spoken so much over my life, but nothing seems to come to pass? Why is it that I know, that I know, that I know you have called me to do something great in this world, but I have yet to accomplish it? When will I walk in my purpose and my destiny? When will my breakthrough come? Why have you connected me with so many influential people, yet I remain in an average position? When will I rise to the top? How much more do I have to go through to get to where you are taking me? Will I be the generation that stops the generational curse? For the very first time in my life, I feel like giving it all up. If this describes you, keep reading. God is not done with you yet.

6

From Desperation to Destiny

I was an abused single mother of six, but there was something inside of me that refused to give up. God took me back to when I was nine. He reminded me that I was the *golden child*. I always knew I was special, but never felt that way. After working a few jobs at temporary services, and only being able to find part-time work, the struggle was still real. I was making it, but still struggling to provide for me and my children. I was attending a local church, and the pastor heard I was having a hard time. The senior pastor reached out to me to let me know that he was aware of what I was going through.

He asked me, "Do you know how to clean?"

I told him, "Yes."

"Do you know how to iron?"

"Yes, but I'm not going to iron a thing." We started laughing.

"I need a new house cleaner because mine quit. How about you come take a look at my house and see if you want to clean it?"

I went to look at his home. It was beautiful and well-maintained. So, I agreed to clean his home in exchange for him paying me a set amount of money at the beginning of each month. This ensured that the kids and I had a roof over our heads and we wouldn't be on the street. At first, I was supposed to clean three times a week, but he decided that was too much. We agreed that I would clean twice a week. Cleaning his home felt so natural and it was very therapeutic. I had found something to ease my mind and give me time to think. So, after faithfully cleaning twice a week for months, the pastor suggested that I start a cleaning business. I told him he'd lost his mind.

So, I took a job doing logistics at Procter & Gamble. I was working full-time during the day, and I still cleaned twice a week at night when I got off work. I hated my job because I realized that I wasn't built for corporate America.

One day, I was cleaning, and the pastor asked me, "Did you start that cleaning business yet?"

"No," I replied.

"You are going to wish you had listened to me one day."

When he said that, it pricked my spirit. I really didn't like my position and what I was doing. I was sitting at my desk and I told God that I needed to find a new job. I was at my wits' end and I wanted a change. Once again, God spoke loud and clear.

"You can either find a new job or you can create them."

It immediately made me think about what the pastor said. I took a leap of *faith* and decided to start a cleaning company. In October of 2014, my cleaning company was birthed. Because of the family that I had married into, I had come to know a lot of prominent people in the city. So, I started reaching out to people, cleaning one house at a time. I called all of my pretty girl friends and asked them to do a photo shoot for my business. I didn't want to look like any other company. I rented a place in Covington,

Kentucky. Then, I created my marketing materials from those photos and my business started to grow.

Within the first three months, I got my first commercial janitorial contract cleaning account. While I now had this 60,000-square-foot facility, the only thing I was missing was cleaning equipment and cleaning chemicals. I found out about some good cleaning vendors. There was only one problem: I didn't have the money that I needed to buy the commercial equipment for the account. In the meantime, I was setting up vendor accounts to order my supplies. I had to be creative. I took $2,000 from my income tax refund check to fund my business. I purchased all the equipment that I needed and bought the necessary cleaning supplies. That money that I took to fund my business brought in $1,500 a month. It was well worth the investment. I usually spent my income tax money on nonsense, but I realized that I really wanted something different out of life. I knew if I wanted something different, I had to do something different.

My business grew faster than I could keep up with, complete with ups and downs. I had my own office space. I had the contract to clean the building my office was in and the one next to it. In the meantime, I was at every event the city had. I took advantage of every networking opportunity. I joined organizations that would give me free advice and help me with business development. I took every class I could to further develop my skills. I had four mentors to help guide me into this thing I wanted called success. I placed myself at events of the power players in the city. I made sure that I stayed at the top of people's minds. If you didn't hear my name, you saw my face. I made it my business to make sure you knew who I was and what I did.

After a year and a half of working my behind off, networking like it was going out of style, and participating in everything I thought would benefit me, my family and my business, I started receiving awards. My organic cleaning company won The New Business of the Year Award from the City of Cincinnati and The Sustainability Award from the City of Cincinnati. In July 2016, one of the local newspapers wrote an article on how this single mom of six took $2,000 and turned it into an award-winning cleaning business. God's hand was moving in my life. My hard work and perseverance were finally paying off.

The Father I Never Knew and a Dream Come True

When I got married in 2010, I realized that I had my father's American name, Hilton.

I never really paid attention to my birth certificate. I only used my birth certificate when it was necessary. I had changed my last name to my then husband's last name at marriage. I told myself I would always keep my last name of the father that I was so desperate to find. In my heart of hearts, I always felt like he was alive. But I was never able to locate him. I find it truly amazing that good can come out of such a bad situation. A local paper featured an article on me and my business on July 5, 2016. That article opened many doors.

On July 21, 2016, a lady by the name of Mary called.

"Hello, is this Christeria M?"

"Who's calling?" I asked.

"My name is Mary. You don't know me, but I am your father's wife."

"Huh? Are you calling from *The Steve Harvey Show*?" I only asked that question because, a couple weeks prior, I'd sent in a request to *The Steve Harvey Show* to help me locate my father.

She said, "No. I don't know who that is. Your father has been looking for you his entire life and he wants to talk to you. He lives in the Dominican Republic and, with your permission, he would like to call you from an 809 telephone number."

I was at the car lot, looking for a new car, when that call came through. I didn't know if I should cry or be overjoyed. I felt every emotion that one would feel after waiting 41 years to speak to their father. My father called me two minutes later, and he cried, and *I cried*. My father explained to me that he never meant to leave me, but he lost touch with my mother.

My father said "When I left to go to New York, I got locked up in prison. I didn't know how to find your mother when I got out. About ten years of getting out of prison, I was deported and had to go back to the Dominican Republic, where I live now."

My father and I called my mom on a three-way call and she couldn't believe that she was actually talking to my father. My mother was in such disbelief, but she was so happy for me. She recognized my father by his voice. I had found the father that I had been looking for my entire life.

My father and I talked almost every day in the beginning. My father told me that I also had three brothers and a sister. He gave me the numbers to all three of my brothers, my sisters and some aunts and uncles so I could reach out. I was so scared. I didn't know what to say or what to expect. *What if they rejected me?* God showed up and showed out in my life. They all knew about me, but they told me no one could find me. I talked to my Aunt GG and she was happy to speak to me. She arranged for me to meet some of my family members. In March 2017, I flew to Tampa to meet my aunts, uncles and cousins. I stayed at their homes, and I was so scared of what I didn't know. They all had big, beautiful homes with lakes and ponds in the back. I couldn't believe this was happening to me. My dream came true.

I could see where some of my ways and beliefs, and my God-given entrepreneurial skills, came from. I visited

Orlando and Tampa. They treated me like royalty. They served me food, took me out to the pier and took really good care of me. I returned home with a new meaning of life, a different view of God and a different view of His grace. I knew this was just the beginning of my journey. I was still in culture shock that I was Dominican. Most of my father's relatives were bilingual and some didn't speak much English. In February 22, 2018, I flew to Boston to meet my four siblings. My brother, JB, and I were the same age, but eight months apart. My brother, SB, was a year younger than me. My brother, BH, was 10 years younger than me, and my sister, AV, was 14 years younger than me. My sister AV was the one who found me. She said, "One night, God woke me up out of my sleep and told me I needed to find my sister. I found you by your business and your last name."

On February 23, 2018, all of my newfound siblings and I came together for the first time. I couldn't believe what God was doing in my life. It all seemed so real. While it took over 41 years to happen, it seemed like I was still dreaming. We went to Beehive in Boston to listen to a live band and enjoy some good food. We had to take some time to just learn more about one another. The night was over way too soon and we had to part ways. I went back to my hotel, and they all went home.

On July 11, 2018, almost two years after I got that first phone call, I flew to meet my father in Punta Cana. My brother, BH, was getting married. My father couldn't leave the Dominican Republic, so that was why my brother got married there. There were so many blessings wrapped up in one trip. I felt like I had hit the jackpot. I met my dad on July 11th and it was a reunion of a lifetime. We hugged and I didn't cry. I was more so overwhelmed than anything. After attending my brother's wedding and staying at the lovely resort, Hard Rock in Punta Cana, it was time to go four days later. I would soon leave the resort to catch a bus to travel two hours to Santa Domingo by myself. They gave me very specific directions to the name of the bus stop and the time of arrival for the bus. I met my dad, my sister, my stepmom, my niece and some other family members in Santa Domingo to prepare to go on our three-hour journey to a small island called Samana.

I spent four days with my father and the rest of the family in Samana. I got to learn more about my father and ask him all the questions that I never got answers to. It was a bittersweet visit because I felt like I'd missed out on so much time that I could never get back. I wasn't angry. I was more so hurt because of the abandonment that I felt deep in my heart. But the more I got to know him, the less angry I was. I learned that this was just the way he was. I'm not condoning his actions or saying it's okay. But it was okay. I was at peace. Samana was a beautiful place and the water was so pretty. It wasn't an economically thriving place, but the people were happy. They were purely happy to be alive and it gave me a new sense of peace. The entire family went to a beach called Playa Rincon. I saw donkeys and poisonous snakes on the beach. Bulls, cows, chickens, roosters and horses freely roamed the streets. *What a wonderful and beautiful experience! God is so, so good*, I kept telling myself. What an awesome God we serve! The best part about it was for me to find out that my paternal side of the family were big believers of Christ. Our genes and our personalities were undeniable.

7

P.E.A.C.E.

Purge

Purge (verb) means: 1. rid (someone) of an unwanted feeling, memory, or condition, typically giving sense of cathartic release. 2. An abrupt or violent removal of a group of people from an organization or place.

At first, I didn't understand what it meant to purge things out of my life. Whatever was happening to me was a compound of what had already happened. I staggered between the past pains, hurt and disappointments and the present pain, hurt and disappointments. I never knew what it was like to self-examine. I needed to see what was broken, what needed to be mended, and what needed to change so my life would change. I realized I had to go back to my childhood, where all of this started. I had to purge the rejection of my mother, the abandonment of my father and the molestation of my stepfather. I had to purge the kidnapping and rape I'd endured by a so-called friend and the abuse at the hands of someone I called husband. I had to let it all go. Every layer and every emotion attached to my past had to go. At this point in my life, it wasn't an option. I could keep going on, repeating the same mistakes, picking the wrong men and making bad decisions that wasn't good for me. I owed it to myself and to my children to give us the life I'd always dreamed of us having.

Rejection had to be replaced with acceptance. Abandonment had to be replaced with redemption. Pain had to be replaced with purpose and hurt had to be replaced with healing. The disappointments had to be replaced with no expectations from people. I had hit rock bottom so many times that I never expected to come up and stay up. My expectations never allowed me to live out my full potential because they kept me stuck in my past. I always wanted to be great, but never thought I could be great because my past told me so. So, I stopped expecting what I wanted others to give me and started giving it to myself. It was a lonely place at first. Then, it was a place to be alone. That place where I could look into the mirror and speak to it. A place where I would have to not only identify everything that hurt me, but also *everyone* who hurt me. That place where I had to forgive those who never apologized and those who weren't sorry. I had to forget about every opportunity I didn't get. But I had to be grateful for every opportunity I did have. I had to accept the fact that you only do better when you know better. Unfortunately, sometimes rejection is part of the process. You will never fit in if you were born to stand out. I had to love myself genuinely like I always wanted and needed to be loved. I had to forgive and love my mother for the things she let happen to me and the ways I felt she rejected me. I had to forgive and love my father like he'd never left me. I had to treat him as if he had always been there for me. I had to tell my baby's daddy, who kidnapped and raped me, how it affected me. Every open wound, I had to work to close with prayer and the Word of God.

    You can never get true healing until you are ready to be real with yourself. I had to take accountability for every mistake I made and every bad decision I made. I had to take accountability for everyone I allowed to treat me wrong and for not standing up for myself. I had to isolate myself and love me, right where I was, broken and all. While I was not perfect, I was better. I was becoming a better person day by day. It was so lonely, but it was so necessary. How could you ever teach someone to love you when you really don't know how to love yourself? I had to learn me and truly love me. I took myself on dates and did the things I always desired to do. I picked myself up and motivated myself because I needed it. I owed it to myself. I had to tune into my children and listen to them because I was always so busy trying to survive instead of taking care of them. I had to instill in my children what I wished was instilled inside of me. I had to accept the fact that some relationships don't die. They just change, and we should be okay with that.

    I had so much work to do on the inside of me. There was no time for anyone else. The more I recognized and acknowledged my flaws and shortcomings, the better I was able to deal with them. There was a peace that I had never experienced. A peace that couldn't be bought, but only earned through complete obedience. A peace that could only come from acknowledgement of your sins and repentance to do better. A peace that I had longed for, but now had found. It was finally happening. I was filled with both good and bad emotions but experiencing the true meaning of joy. The only people I had expectations from was myself and God. I had to seek God in everything. Things no longer had to go my way because I had learned to replace my will with His will. I petitioned to God my dreams, goals and aspirations. I asked Him to direct my steps. I asked God to show me the hearts of everyone around me and remove the people who were not meant for me. I asked God to give me the strength to let go and let God. I asked God to use me to help other single mothers, but to guide me in doing so. I told God to bring out everything in me that hurt me and use it to heal me. I reflected, reorganized and redirected my steps with God's orders.

    I let God strategically place people in my path, but I asked God to give me the sight to see who they were sent by. The things that used to be difficult became easy. The people who I once thought were sent to break me only made me into who God called me to be. With every new challenge that came into my life, I asked myself, "What can

I learn from it?"

So many bad things happen to good people, and so many good things happen to bad people. Every failed relationship is an opportunity to start fresh. Every opportunity missed is a chance to get prepared and stay prepared. Every bad thing can be used to help change someone else's life. The purge was real, but so was the process. Anything worth having is worth fighting for.

I was worth the fight and so were my children. To be great in life, I'd experienced a multitude of good and bad experiences. I saw my light but needed it to be recognized. Most diamonds come from underneath the ground and have been covered by dirt. Then, they're extracted from what was and impacted by what's to be. Every diamond with clarity, no matter the size, has to go through the process and through the fire. I realized that I was a diamond in the rough. I had been through the fire and been through the process. Now, it was time to be great.

Remember when I told you we moved back home to Ohio? God placed Genesis 12:2-3 in my spirit. I forgot that while I was going through the process, but God brought it back to my remembrance.

"Just because God shows you who you are, doesn't mean you're ready for it."
~T.D. Jakes

Erase Pride

The Bible says, *Pride goes before destruction, a haughty spirit before a fall* (Proverbs 16:18). I've learned that a closed mouth doesn't get fed. You'll never get what you want if you're too afraid to ask for it. You'll never get what you need if you're too afraid to admit you need it. You never know who or where your blessing is going to come from. Sometimes, your blessing lies in you just opening up your mouth. The Bible says, *Ask, and it shall be given to you; seek and you shall find; knock and it will be opened for you. For everyone who asks receives, and he who seeks finds, and to him who knocks it will be opened* (Matthew 7:7-8). I often went through unnecessary trials and tribulations because I let my past experiences affect my current circumstances. Getting rid of pride was not an easy thing for me to do but suffering because I didn't want to humble myself was harder.

Being vulnerable to the right person is scary, but it can be very rewarding. There were so many things and resources I needed and didn't have. But I couldn't obtain them due to my prideful ways. As I was purging all the hurts and pains, I also purged my pride. I learned it is okay to *not* be okay. Healing comes with acknowledgment and truth. There was so much healing that my heart, mind and body was longing for. Even though I got rid of my pride, I had to maintain my strength. I also understood that just because someone smiled in my face didn't mean they were genuinely happy for me. I had to be careful who I opened up to and even more careful who I became vulnerable around. Anytime someone new came into my life, I always asked God to show me their heart before I would give them mine. My heart was fragile and so were my emotions. I couldn't trust them with just anyone. I had to embrace where I was, but I knew where I desired to be. I had to get rid bad of habits, bury impulsive thoughts that stunted my growth and strengthen my self-praise. I had to identify what kept me broken, bound and wounded for so long.

I turned what used to be pride into praise. The only way you fail is if you never try. They say to get something you've never had, you have to do something you've never done. ~Author Unknown

My entire life, I lived with the secret struggles that hindered me from getting to where I wanted to be. I never said a word because I was used to never having a voice. When I spoke my truth, no one believed me. I've learned that whether people believe you or not, never be afraid to speak your truth and stand in it. You have one voice. It's imperative that you use it. Sometimes when you speak, you not only speak for yourself, but serve as a voice for others. Being able to seek help is one thing, but being able to *accept help* is another.

Pride leaves you hungry in more than one way. Sometimes, we miss opportunities because we're afraid to ask for them. Relationships stay stagnant because we choose not to forgive. Our dreams go unfulfilled because we would rather be served than to serve. We pretend everything is fine, but everything is not okay. Letting go of pride is hard and sometimes difficult to do. At the end of the day, no one wants to look like a fool. No one wants to feel rejected. You don't want to think that you look stupid. Forgive because you have been forgiven. Forgiving others gives you the power of peace. You no longer care what anyone thinks of you because what you need is more important than what someone thinks. The only dumb question is the one that you never ask. You never know who may say, "Yes!" when you thought they would say, "No."

My life changed when I humbled myself. I apologized for the pain that I had caused others, known and unknown. I told people that I was working on me and becoming a better me. I wasn't afraid to say that I'm not perfect. When I needed help, I asked for it. Ten thousand people declining you will never supersede the one acceptance. Imagine how much further you could be if you were willing to ask for a hand, regardless of what someone thought of you. For me, it was one of the hardest things I ever had to do, but also the most rewarding. When people knew my story, when they knew that I had six children, they often pitched in to give me a helping hand. The heart and the hand of God always moved in my life. Ask yourself a few questions:

1. Do you have a true sensible assessment of who you are? If so, who?

   _____
   _____
   _____
   _____
   _____

2. Do you have a true sensible assessment of what you really need to move forward in life?

   _____
   _____
   _____
   _____
   _____

3. Who are you willing to be vulnerable to?

   _____
   _____
   _____
   _____
   _____

4. What can I ask someone right now that would help elevate me to the next level or place in life?

_____
_____
_____
_____
_____

5. Are you willing to sacrifice your time in exchange for someone else's experience?

_____
_____
_____
_____
_____

Action

Taking action is one of those things that you hear people talk about often, but many seldom do. Everyone wants what they want, but few are willing to go get it. Action speaks louder than words. Put in the work and don't expect handouts. You can show people better than you can tell them. When it's time to take action, have a set plan in place for the action. Make goals for yourself and the things you want to accomplish in life. Set daily goals. This could be simply getting all of your affairs in order or tying up some loose ends. Set weekly goals, which pretty much entails things that you would like to get accomplished that week, but not necessarily in one day. Also set monthly goals. You may want to make a certain amount of revenue and/or money per month. That would mean identifying areas of opportunity for you to earn money or generate more revenue. Then, set short-term goals and long-term goals.

A short-term goal is something like starting a business, working your way out of the company or being able to take a cruise to a place you've always desired to go to. A long-term goal is something that may take longer to acquire. Your long-term goal may be to become a millionaire, to become a billionaire, to graduate from college, to have a certain dollar amount in the bank or to write a book. These goals should be specific and results-driven. I purchased a $15 journal to keep track of my daily and weekly goals. Every time I hit one of my goals, I highlighted it and put the date next to it. Every day of my journal also has a date. This is because I wanted to measure and follow my success. The more you can see what you're getting accomplished, the more likely you will be to get more accomplished.

It may start off as a habit. But, the more you do it, it becomes a lifestyle. Most successful people are successful because they have mastered what they do with their time. Time management is one of the keys to success. The next step of action is to invest in a coach. Someone once asked me, "What is the best investment you've ever made?" My response was, "The investment in myself." Every time I got extra money, I found new ways to invest in me and new ways to become a better me. I've invested in many classes, coaches and paid networking events. The investment increased my skill set, my business acumen, and my personal and professional growth.

I am now doing the things that I love and getting paid in the process. I've learned to monetize my time. If people are not willing to pay for your time, they are not your client. Once you get a clear picture of your future, you have to do the things that are required to create that future. I always wanted to give my children the life I dreamed of having. They say you only live once. If you do it right, once is all you need. I had personal and professional goals for myself. Reaching those goals was never *optional*. I was creating my future and my children's future. We can't choose the hand we are dealt in life, but we can choose how we play our cards.

My challenge for you is to design your roadmap for life and stay on course. Most importantly, stay in your lane. If you don't know where to start, find someone who can get you moving in the right direction. Research and reflect as much as possible. Don't be afraid to make mistakes. Your last mistake is going to be your best teacher. Move slowly, but strategically. Don't make impulsive moves, but rather sound decisions. Don't be afraid to take risks. The bigger the risks, often the better the rewards. Never minimize your dreams and goals. Be yourself, not who someone else thinks you should be. Stay true and real with yourself at all times, even if you can't stay true and real with someone else. My goal was to *impact*, not to *impress*! What's yours? Take these steps below and watch how your life changes!

1. Understand who you are called to be in life.
2. If you don't understand who you are called to be at this point in life, identify who you would like to be.
3. Write the vision of what you *think* it takes to get there. Oftentimes, what we think and what it actually takes to achieve our goals are two different things.
4. Associate with like-minded people.
5. Get a mentor and a coach. Oftentimes, these are different people. You should have more than one of each.
6. Learn something new and learn something different.
7. Understand your skills, talents and/or gifts, and monetize them.
8. Find out what you're good at. What comes naturally?
9. Find an organization to enhance your skills and your business acumen.
10. Visualize yourself where you desire to be.
11. Build relationships with new people, especially people who are doing the things you desire to do.
12. Get rid of all unhealthy relationships and/or anything that subtracts from you.

13. Read, read, read, read and *read*. The more you read, the more you grow.
14. Speak affirmations over your life daily. For everything that you are not, speak what you desire to be. Do this three times a day, every day, until you believe what you are speaking. Some examples are: "I am successful. I am free. I am delivered. I am a winner. I am healthy. I am whole. I am abundant. I am who God called me to be. I have no lack." Your affirmations can be anything you choose to speak, but they have to be positive.
15. Commit to yourself for yourself.
16. Get an accountability partner.

Changed Mind

> "When the pain of remaining the same becomes greater than the pain of changing, we will change."
>
> ~Tony Robins

I was tired of the same old, same old. I had big dreams, but little support for me and my children. I felt like I had failed myself and my children in so many ways. I wanted something that no one around me had. I was willing to do the things that no one around me was doing.

I knew I wanted to live like only the 2% of America could. So, I had to write the vision and make it plain. How do you get what you never had, and become who you desire to be, when you don't know where to start? It's not easy, but it's possible.

After you purge the old and accept the new, ask for what you want and have the heart to go after it. When your mindset shifts, so does your life. If your mindset shifts for the better, your life shifts for the better. If your mindset shifts for the worst, your life shifts for the worst. Study those you desire to be like only to implement what you've learned, not to duplicate who they are. Recognize what has held you back from where you always wanted to be, then bury that thing. If it was fear, replace it with stupid faith. If it's pride, replace it with humility. If it was impulsive decisions and behaviors, become more rigid and sound. While it's easier said than done, it can be done. If you want something bad enough, you'll do whatever it takes.

Your mind changes when you decide that it's okay for it to change. When you become tired of being tired, you look for new ways to have peace. For me, a simple form of *desperation* led to a journey of *destiny*. No one around me could see my dream. But that didn't matter. Life is about taking those risks for a dream that no one can see but *you*. Just because people don't see your dream doesn't mean you're not supposed to go after it. It just means that you don't expose your vision to everyone. Outside of someone who is willing and ready to invest in you, never try to convince someone of what you know you are called to be and to do. Replace any negative thought with a positive thought. Words of affirmation and positive thinking plays a huge part of your success. It's part of the purging process and changes you for the better. Be realistic. You can only have what you truly believe you can achieve. If your heart is telling you one thing, and your mind is telling you something else, the two are in conflict with one another. The heart and mind should align with each other. Believe in what you're going after. Most importantly, believe that you can achieve it. If you believe it, you can achieve it. It's so cliché, but it's true. How can you convince someone else to believe in you if you don't believe in yourself? Identify what needs to change in your life. Who do you need to get out of your life to make the necessary changes?

Here are some more questions that I challenge you to answer:

1. Why is change necessary?

   _____
   _____
   _____
   _____
   _____

2. How does change align with your future?

   _____
   _____
   _____
   _____
   _____

3. What is necessary for you to change in your life?

   _____
   _____
   _____
   _____
   _____

4. What do you fear most about changing?

   _____
   _____
   _____
   _____
   _____

5. What skills or personal growth do you need to level up?

   _____
   _____
   _____
   _____
   _____

6. What are your next steps?

   _____
   _____
   _____
   _____
   _____

7. What lessons have you learned?

   _____
   _____
   _____
   _____
   _____

8. What does success look like for you?

   _____
   _____
   _____
   _____
   _____

9. How do you plan to achieve the success you envision?

   _____
   _____
   _____
   _____
   _____

Evolve

When you know better, you do better. When you learn more, you often become more of what you learn. To evolve is simply to change or develop slowly often into a better, more complex, or more advanced state. Knowledge is power. But it is only power if you use it. Let me remind you of the actions that truly help you evolve to your full potential. Forgive those who hurt you, even if they never apologized. Be true to yourself, even if you can't be true to anyone else. Stay in your lane so you don't get off course. Never try to convince someone of your worth because that means they don't see your value. It's hard to walk in purpose when you don't understand what your purpose is. Seek purpose daily. Wash off the proclivities that reflect your history. Everything is not meant to be fixed. Feed what you desire and bury what you don't.

Take one step at a time. Don't look for an elevator. Don't be afraid to fail. Failure is part of the process, not the end of the process. The more you give, the more you receive. Be willing to sit under those who you want to learn from. Don't be afraid to take risks because that's where your rewards come from. Let your past be the lesson that your future may present so you can pass any test going forward. Anything that subtracts from you is usually not good for you. Never worry about your competition. Your only competition is *you*. Celebrate every small win. Remember, for every closed door, there is always an opened one. Don't try to force what's meant to remain shut. If you learn how to make $100,000, you can make $1 million dollars. The process is called duplication. Never be afraid to start over.

Be conscious of the company you keep. Live within your means and think big. It's a lifestyle.

Every decision you make has a consequence, good or bad. Be wise about the decisions you make. Research and reflect as much as possible. No matter how hard it gets, don't give up. I've *purged,* erased my *pride,* launched into *action* and *changed* my old ways. Now, I'm evolving and have my *eye on my future*. I've unlearned so much along the way, but I've learned so much more. It's not the destination that gives us the greatest joy. It's the journey.

God often places us in situations and places that we have no desire to be in. It's up to us to learn from those situations and not repeat the same mistakes. It's one thing to go through. It's another thing when you put yourself through. I put myself through a whole lot of unnecessary stuff. Keep that in mind as you move forward with greatness. Along the way, I've learned simple is best. Great things come with time. Patience is of the virtue. Fear limits you and the truth really does set you free. Honesty builds long-lasting relationships. Your word will take you further in life than your dollar can. Everything is not what it appears to be, and everybody is not who they say they are. Never focus on who people say they are and what they do. Remain focused on you.

I no longer focused on what I didn't have. I learned to focus on what I wanted and how to obtain it. The more I focused on the good, the more good I received. I kept my dreams and visions to myself because I knew in my heart that everyone was not rooting for me. I stopped signing up for things that I knew I couldn't finish and or things I truly had no interest in. I learned that it was okay to say, "No!" and to be okay with the truth. I stayed in when everyone else was going out. I found comfort in the uncomfortable places. That's where real growth comes from.

Most millionaires have seven streams of income. Billionaires simply learn how to multiply what they do and have. Peter Ducker says, "The best way to predict your future is to create it." So, I created my future. I made a budget for my dreams and found the people who could help me achieve them. Most of my dreams were out of my budget, but within my reach. Never be afraid to reach for the sky. I also learned that God never gives you a vision that's in your budget. If your vision is in your budget, then it's probably too small.

I always knew I was created to do more. I felt called to help others accomplish their dreams and build their enterprises. I'm maximizing my full potential and helping others do the same. Christeria Lynn, LLC, is a business development and consulting company that assists new entrepreneurs with launching their businesses. I also assist existing entrepreneurs with operations, branding and marketing. I have since founded a non-profit organization called B.H.E.R.R.D., Inc., which is my true passion and calling in life.

B.H.E.R.R.D. is a non-profit that is dedicated to helping single mothers in achieving their dreams and goals. We assist single mothers with the challenges of life that hinder them from getting the most out of life. Our focus is to create financial stability, self-sufficiency and opportunities for growth and abundance. B.H.E.R.R.D.'s vison is to change the world—one single mother at a time. Just call me the Six Figures Single Mom of Six™. The oldest of four siblings, and born with all odds against me, I managed to thrive and succeed. If I can do it, so can you. I am now an author, motivational speaker and business coach. At one point, I didn't think I would ever be able to see past my pain. As I applied P.E.A.C.E. (Purge, Erase Pride, Action, Changed Mind and Evolve) to my life, the pain became my past. My future was bright. Everything that I dreamed of doing and becoming started to come to pass. It's one thing when we try to do it on our own. It's another when we sit back and trust God to do it for us.

Let me remind you. I am a single mother of six. Once rejected and abandoned, I've been molested by a loved one, kidnapped and raped, and emotionally and physically beaten. Today, I am healed. I was forced to leave my job with $125.32 in my bank account. I opened up my own real estate brokerage two years later. I took $2,000 from my income tax refund check and turned it into an award-winning cleaning business. In February of 2017, I started Christeria Lynn, LLC.

My life changed when I decided that it was okay for it to change. My life changed when I changed the way that I looked at the things that happened in my life. My life changed when I learned to truly trust God and walk in obedience. Change comes from within. Now every trial is a new chapter for my next book.

ABOUT THE AUTHOR

Christeria is a single mother of six beautiful children, five girls and one boy. When she is not pursuing her career endeavors, Christeria enjoys traveling, listening to music, reading, shopping and spending time with her children. Christeria makes her home in the Atlanta area.

Connect with her online at www.christerialynn.com.

ChristeriaLynn   ChristeriaLynn

ChristeriaLyn   ChristeriaLynn

The birthing of this book was assisted by:

The Literary Midwife

Helping you get your book from your heart to your reader's hands.
www.hagarfoh.org/literary-midwife

Made in the USA
Columbia, SC
15 September 2019